You Ain't Going Crazy Darling!

Narcissistic Patterns

Mel John

ISBN: 978-1-914439-08-7

DEDICATION

This book is dedicated to all the survivors of narcissistic abuse, those who are still trying to escape narcissistic abuse and those who are not quite sure if they need to run for the hills!

This is the reason I will donate 20% of the sales of my book to a charity that can help victims of coercive behaviors. And if there isn't one available, I will make it my mission to build a charity from scratch.

CONTENTS

Hey little fighter, soon things will be brighter.

"The first step in healing from narcissistic abuse is, realising that you have been abused. You have to accept that they were putting on an act. You were dealing with a very disordered individual. They function in life and in their relationships by way of manipulation and corruption. They don't know any other way. This is who they are. They are wired differently and they see people as puppets for their own entertainment and use. You have to accept that this was not your fault, and that this is the way they relate to everyone. They are sadistic people who can't handle anyone being happier or better than them. Get out and go, "no contact." You didn't break them and you absolutely can't fix them. But they definitely could and will break you if you stay."

-Maria Consiglio @understandingthenarc

ACKNOWLEDGMENTS

Thank you to Donna Dyer and the memory of your beautiful Daughter Linzi Thorne for all your help and I hope your suffering eases when the truth finally reveals itself.

Thank you to Maria Consiglio @understandingthenarc for all your memes that I found such a great help and inspiration when I was learning about Narcissism.

And most of all a massive thank you to my children, my Daughter Lexie and her partner Dai and my Son Robbie and his Girlfriend Meg. I appreciate you being there for me throughout the drama and helping me find my strength again. I love you with all my heart.

INTRODUCTION

No names are mentioned in this book. No intentions to harm or slander anyone. Actual events are stated to bring awareness to narcissistic abuse. **I was brought up with integrity, don't do to others what you wouldn't want done to yourself.** I have questioned myself and nearly backed out of it. But, since hearing all the horror stories of trauma left after narcissistic abuse (some are horrifically cruel, sometimes lasting for years) I felt if I was my younger self, I would want to be warned about the covert narcissists that walk amongst us daily. I see posts appear from youngsters (female and male) and I can feel their frustration. I can see clearly now how the victims don't understand what's happening to them, and why they're hurting. They're upset, confused and just hoping the toxic relationship will go back to how it used to be in the beginning...if only they knew how.

This era of social media and dating is a virtual playground for a narcissist. If I help more people to become aware, together we may be able to help someone we identify might be a victim, from their posts on social media... even if it's a quick, *are you ok?*

In a nutshell, if I can help even one person spot the signs and listen to their gut feeling, their intuition, (life's whispers as I like to call them) writing this book will all be worthwhile.

1

WHO IS MEL?

I'm a 49 year old mother of two beautiful grown up children, 27 and 21 years of age. Born and bred in Swansea, South Wales, I run my own business from home as a freelance Retrofit & Energy Assessor and have been self-employed for a number of years. I'm a bit of a tomboy at heart- licensed to drive Lorries and motorbikes and had a lovely motorbike for about six years; as a summer rider only.

I had a varied childhood, moved houses regularly (26 last count) and I was in my 3rd school by the time I was six. Thankfully, I was fortunate enough to stay at Dumbarton House School from the age of six to fourteen going on fifteen. My father and mother divorced, our home was repossessed along with most of our furniture. I moved to a council house with my mum, my brother, who is a year younger and my sister, who is six years younger. I spent one year in mainstream school, which wasn't the greatest experience after private education, but I met some great people there and am still in touch with some of them today...in fact one of the girls is now my sister in law.

Money was tight for my mum as she was working two jobs trying to make ends meet. Mum found me a little job, babysitting for her new friend who was married with two kids across the road from ours.

I'm not going to go into details, I'll cut this bit of back story to very basic. I was fourteen going on fifteen, the husband of the lady across the road attempted to abuse me. Luckily I fought and got away. I wasn't believed and was sent back there to babysit. He attempted to rape me the next time, but I fought like an animal and I got away again. Scared, confused and a terrified teenager, I was angry with everyone at that point. I told myself, *the* truth will come out one day. I wasn't believed and I had to move out of my home.

Now, somewhere around that time, I decided I was going to make myself happy. From that day forward, I turned what was a very negative time in my life into a positive one. I told myself every day, *I am lucky, I got away, I am happy* and never spoke about what nearly happened to me again.

Just before my sixteenth birthday I met a lovely guy, who took me under his wings, became my boyfriend and we lived together for a while. We're still friends to this day, even though we don't see each other regularly. He saved me at that time.

At seventeen I bought a small house and at eighteen, I met the father of my children. We were together for twelve years and had two beautiful kids. We split up when I was thirty...that was my doing and I fully hold my hands up to that. As time has passed we have become really good friends and even spend family occasions together. This makes life so much easier all round...especially when the children were growing up.

At thirty two years old, I wanted a business I could run and still take my kids to school and pick them up from school every day. Whilst I worked as a bookkeeper doing the accounts for my uncle's scrap yard, I observed my friend working on a burger van. I was drawn in by the freedom of hours it gave. So, one Friday after work, I drove from Swansea to Plymouth, did a cracking little deal on a small burger van and drove through the night towing it home at 50mph, with help from a friend...longest night of my life,.

Lexie's Burger Van was opened, my friend came to work for me and showed me what to do and thirteen years later I sold the business. Amazing time and I made some great lifelong friends. I even won an award in the Jack Swan Awards for Best Burger Van 2016. Felt absolutely amazing to win that.

When I was 38 and still running my burger van business, the man from twenty three years before, who no one would believe my story about....the man I said I'd never speak of again...yes, that one...his face was plastered all over the newspapers for raping eleven little girls. By the time it got to court it was nine young girls. All of them were young women at this point.

Brave beautiful women traumatised for the rest of their lives by what they had endured by a very sick individual.

I was one of those witnesses testified in court. The man was sentenced to the maximum of fifteen years in prison. I found out on the day of sentencing that I was the only one who had managed to escape. I was very lucky and always grateful for the strength I found to escape all those years earlier. But the guilt of not trying harder to get someone to believe me all those years ago, consumed me. *Maybe I could have saved those young girls, if I'd been believed*. I tortured myself for years with what ifs.

In the end, I chose to heal by telling myself daily, *I am lucky, I got away, I am happy*, over and over. A positive mental attitude has definitely helped me overcome things over the years and I'll tell you more about what has actually helped me to overcome things later in this book.

At this stage I will admit that the pressure of the court case at 38 years old and hearing the horrific things that had happened to the ladies when they were children had a much more traumatic effect, than I realised...or would admit to. I just put a brave face on, a big smile and tried to block it all out once again.

When I sold my little burger business, I found myself at a total crossroads...Jack of all trades, master of......? *Hmmm... do I go back to being a beauty therapist? No! A lorry driver? No! Accounts technician? No, not sure which path to take*. Then out of the blue I was asked to go to Milton Keynes England, for a weekend to help out with work, which turned into 3 months of work.

I love driving, so when I returned to Wales, I bought a van and did delivery driving for Amazon at Christmas time. I then went on to buy a franchise with a delivery company and drove a big long wheel base Mercedes van for a couple of months.

I was happy enough but I knew there was more I could do...I could feel it, yet I couldn't find it. I wanted to learn a new trade, something I could scale, and something I would enjoy and love. Along comes my lifelong friend, just at the right time. He recommended I went on some courses which I had to fund myself, learn a new skill and get qualified and he would have plenty of work lined up for me. I did and I've never looked back. In fact, I'm quite addicted to taking new courses and sitting exams now. I love my work and feel very lucky and fortunate that I've been able to learn a new skill at my age. Plus, I get to meet lovely new people along the way.

2

LISTEN TO THE RED FLAGS

"Listen to the red flags, gut feelings and intuition. They are always telling you the truth."- **Mel John**

Unless you've been involved with a narcissistic person, you will never understand the pain and hurt they cause. It is soul destroying. You end up questioning your very thoughts and even your own sanity. Narcissists are the cruelest, most evil people whose main intention is to destroy another person's life. Even the strongest of characters can be fooled. I have written this book to try and help others spot the warning signs early and not to trust the words of another...only their actions.

I am therefore committed to raise awareness of narcissistic behavior and personality disorders. There are multiple suicides due to victims not being believed, and no one understanding what they have endured at the hands of these monsters who walk among us. One seldom comprehends the extent and type of abuse that actually goes on behind closed doors. It's one of the hardest forms of abuse to explain and prove and unless you have actually been through it or actually learnt about it, it would never make sense to you. It's a veritable impossibility to understand the mental abuse and trauma that victims suffer at the hands of narcissists. It's like trying to explain colour to a colour blind person.

Searching for answers as to why my ex-fiancé could be so calculating, so malicious, so devious and downright nasty behind closed doors, (whilst I made excuses for his vile behaviour and put it down to grief), I discovered patterns.

The narcissistic patterns I discovered, I could finally put a name to! I experienced them all in my past 3 relationships: **mirroring, love bombing, future faking, theft, fraud, ghosting, gas lighting, flying monkeys**. I am sure it might not be making much sense to you. They didn't make any sense to me either and because I'm a truth seeker (which tends to get me into trouble even at my age) I had to figure it out.

I am aware that publishing this book, is going to provoke the narcissist in question even further. I'm already handling his disgusting smear campaign, but his web of lies will unravel as the truth always comes out in the end, no matter how long it takes. I owe it to you, to tell you my story, so you will know that you ain't going crazy darling, when he/she tries to tell you so.

I could have ended up mentally unstable and financially ruined, if his plan had fallen into place. So, if this book helps, even one person to take their time and really get to know someone, and not fall for false promises, to actually trust in consistent actions and NEVER just words...I will be absolutely over the pigging moon!!!

The main aim is that those of you who are in relationships with a narcissist, who feel trapped and find it hard to explain what is going on, will hopefully resonate with parts of my story. I made it my mission to find out and learn as much as I could so I could process what my last relationship was all about, why I felt so drained, and physically sick around certain people in his life. And how lucky was I to discover the REAL truth in what was actually a very short space of time! I'll share what I did to help me find my strength, from my daily routines, to YouTube videos and more.

"I'M NOT CRYING BECAUSE OF YOU: YOU'RE NOT WORTH IT. I'M CRYING BECAUSE MY DELUSION OF WHO YOU WERE WAS SHATTERED BY THE TRUTH OF WHO YOU ARE."
–DR. STEVE MARABOLI

thisislovelifequotes.net

3

SPOT THE SIGNS

"Not everyone who gets into an abusive relationship is insecure, timid and lacks self-esteem. Some are strong, confident, successful people who were manipulated into relationships with devious people. People who took advantage of their goodness and beat them down so bad they forgot how to love themselves." **MARIA CONSIGLIO.**

Each time I didn't learn my lesson I ended up with the worst kind of narcissist. I would ask myself the same questions over and over again. ***What have I done again?*** The closeted sociopath, covert narcissist...they all made a bee line for me. ***My choice in men is atrocious****, I would think.* But I did not seem to have the answer.

Now, I'm not a qualified psychiatrist or doctor, but someone who has learnt from experience and much research and wants to help and warn others that not everyone is who they seem to be. My ex-fiancé was the kind who wore a mask in public, the loudest, funniest, charming businessman. He appears happy all the time, everyone likes him, the charmer, and the comedian- but behind closed doors, the mask comes off and he starts his torturous, sick, mind games. I was lucky enough to get away before he got physically abusive, but the day he hurt my dog was the day I left and I never looked back.

Some of his ex-partners were not so lucky-including his ex-wife. Does this sound familiar? Days of mental pressure, feeling like you are going crazy, torture- like your head is in the fast spin cycle of a washing machine. Then there are the rollercoaster days...one day you're feeling on top of the world, he's so kind and saying all the right things, next day, it's like you're dancing with the Devil himself. His moods swing without warning and he is suddenly cruel and nasty to the core. Then as if like magic, once he sees you're upset, he's elated!!! Mission accomplished. Have you been there? I sure have!

But he is not finished with you yet. So the next day he goes overboard with niceness- the charm offensive-making sure you don't leave him!! It's all "crazy making". I was questioning my own sanity, second guessing everything, feeling emotionally drained, but could not quite explain it. Eventually, realising it was all about him wanting to control every part of my life and if I didn't play ball, which I didn't at first, he would torture my mind until I gave into his sick circus of a life. Drained my energy so much I actually thought I'd never be my happy go lucky self again.

A covert narcissist personality is so exact that it is scary. Extreme selfishness, pathological liars, manipulative, deceitful, secretive, love power and control, no conscience, no remorse, no empathy and hurting you makes them feel good. All the while they masquerade in public like a good person.

Every trait describes the devil himself, yet in modern day society we gave him/her/them the name narcissism.

Credit: @THRIVING.AFTER.THE. NARCISSIST

Straight talking and keeping a journal saved me from years of torture, mental abuse and financial loss. Plus, it all helped me to write this book as well. I started with an Instagram page @narcissistic_patterns originally to vent my hurt trying to comprehend what had happened. How could I have been so foolish to be duped by such a twisted and evil man, *were there any other people who had witnessed this kind of "crazy making"?* I wondered to myself all the time. Then the lightbulb moment finally arrives!! Narcissistic personality disorder!! The patterns are all the same.

Omg! Narcissists come in all shapes, sizes, genders & backgrounds in the form of boyfriends, girlfriends, husbands, wives, mothers, fathers, sisters, brothers, bosses, official leaders etc. The one thing that is constant with all the different forms of narcissistic abuse is, there is no empathy... absolute zero. You will drive yourself wild if you think you can help this kind of person to become a better version of themselves as they are totally incapable of any kind of empathy. They can't see that they do any wrong at all, they actually believe their lies and usually surround themselves with their so called "flying monkeys" or enablers who hang off their every word, totally unaware that they too are being manipulated.

What are flying monkeys? These are people in your world whom the Covert Narcissists utilise.

Covert narcissists are grooming their "monkeys" from the outset and they do it very cleverly, you have no idea. It's the little comments, "I have to check everything is ok with the order as my wife is very fussy," in this self-deprecating funny way that makes it known that you are demanding and difficult to please. "I always do most of the cooking because she is usually tired." On the surface it seems almost nice, even understanding. Yet it's designed to point out to the "monkeys" that you are lazy. That's what they'll remember.

WARNING SIGNS

"Their Poor Me Pity Story."

"Psychopaths know that the best way to exploit empathic people is to take advantage of our natural desire to help and care for others. They do this by orchestrating not one, but many pity plays. They fabricate illnesses; they describe fake injuries; they lie about being the victims of theft, car accidents, and various other disasters; and they lament about how their "crazy ' exes broke their hearts-hearts they don't actually have. They deliberately spin their tales of woe in order to cement the psychopathic bond that they've created by love bombing and flattering us. They use pity plays to portray a facade of real humanity and emotional depth. They pretend to be good people going through rough times, and this is how they are able to manipulate anyone who is kind and loving. So BEWARE of the "poor me" routine. As Martha Stout writes, *"The most reliable sign, the most universal behaviour of unscrupulous people is not directed, as one might imagine, at our fearlessness. It is perversely an appeal to our sympathy."*

Learn the signs. Find your freedom." **Credit: PsychopathFree.com**

Warning sign- If you feel totally drained and exhausted when you're in the company of certain people, be very aware...the mask of the narcissist is slipping. Start running and don't look back, no matter what sob stories they give you...and they will! They will give Oscar winning performances on how sorry they are, they didn't mean to, they'll never do it again, how much they love you, they've never felt that way before...all that nonsense.

If you are a genuinely nice, friendly, caring, empathic and loving person, who wears their heart on their sleeve and tries to see the best in everyone... you are a sitting duck for a narcissist. Be very careful who you trust and who you share your energy with, because that is like blood to a vampire and they will put out all the stops to get you in their clutches and drain your energy completely.

Hopefully you can learn from my mistakes, observe the red flags, and listen to your gut feeling, and not empty words, which is what I did far too quickly after meeting my ex. I foolishly let myself be rushed. So, another lesson learnt was to set healthy boundaries for myself.

4

THE BACK STORY

NARCISSISISTIC ABUSE IN A NUTSHELL

"YOU'RE TRICKED INTO THINKING YOU'VE FOUND YOUR SOULMATE, WHEN ACTUALLY YOU'VE MET THE PERSON WHO WILL BE THE CAUSE OF SOME OF THE LOWEST MOMENTS OF YOUR LIFE."

@recoveringirlfriendromnarcabuse

Now you can skip this section and get straight to the narc bit if you want to...but I found in trying to make sense of the crazy stuff, I had to go back in my mind and try to figure it all out. It might help you too. *Had I already met my Mr. Right and sabotaged it with my lack of self-love*? I really had to question myself. Do you find yourself doing that too when you face these situations?

I had a 13-year relationship with the father of my children, that broke up 18 years ago and now we are great friends and it shows in our amazing kids...well they're 27 and 21 now ...but always my babies. Luckily, we made sure through all our differences and arguments, to pull together and always speak decently about each other, to our kids.

As you can already imagine these past 18 years, have been quite colourful and dramatic, with some really funny, lovely experiences followed by some not so lovely times. But no matter what, my kids always came first. But wow...I often ask myself, what the f*** was I thinking when it came to relationships?

Each time I would fall in love (and I fell hard) - hopeless romantic, idealist, fantasy, you name it! I dreamed of the Knight in shining armour, happy ever after and a blissfully happy life...but that never happened. Can you relate? Do you find yourself to be ever the optimist in relationships, whilst being prepared to sacrifice and overlook just to have that happily ever after that seems to be always just an arm's reach away?

Do you always feel like you are on the outside looking in on the life you imagined but just cannot enter and make it yours?

On reflection, I have had three definite narcissistic partners in my time who will be known as Narc1, Narc2 and Narc3 in chronological order. Two of them had high narcissistic tendencies and one was a covert narcissist. (the devil in disguise) I kept picking them...well they actually came and found me. Now I'm writing it down for you to learn from my experiences. When I was on the downward spiral of one abusive relationship after another, I didn't learn my lesson. I did not understand the first time I was in a relationship with a Narcissist, so the cycle repeated, getting worse each time!!

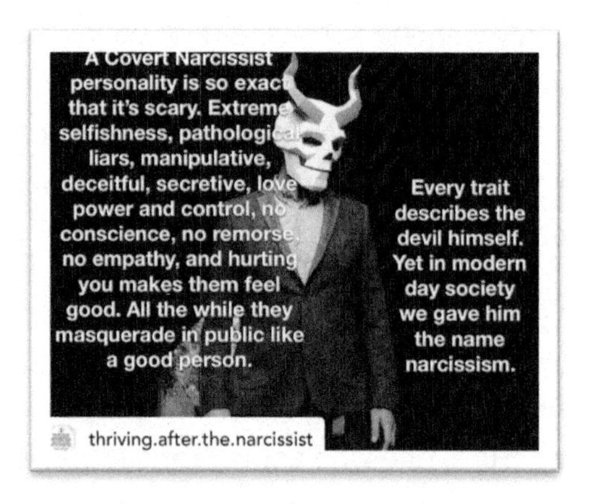

Covert narcissists premeditate to get their supply. They pre-plan from the offset, it is premeditated emotional fraud. Leading to financial and sexual fraud. The manipulation should be made a criminal offense.

NARC1

From the age of 40 – 42 I endured a relationship with NARC1. He put me in hospital. I discovered he'd hurt 3 other women who were scared to come forward. I also later found out his nickname was "Sycho"!! The hospital contacted the police and there was a court case. My kids, the father of my kids and myself were all threatened. It was a terrifying time of my life. I couldn't physically go to work to run my business. Luckily, I had great ladies working for me who stepped up and ran my business for me. As my medical records mysteriously vanished on the day of court hearing, he was convicted only for criminal damage. Thankfully he was given a lifetime restraining order. That's as much as I can discuss on that as it's like prodding a rattle snake just mentioning it.

NARC2- The Nicest of the Narcissists

I met Narc2 when I was aged 43 and we were together for 4 years. He is one who could probably save himself with therapy and cutting out alcohol - also a lesson for myself, to know my limits. He was amazing in bed though...stayed longer than I should, for totally the wrong reasons. His greatest talent? He could ignore and give the silent treatment for 5 days to 2 weeks and nothing would budge him. Walking on eggshells, as I didn't understand narcissistic patterns at the time, I just thought he was really moody so I just cracked on and did my own thing until his drunken rage eased. He had the tongue of a scorpion (and he was a Scorpio star sign), his words were evil and would cut to the core, very nasty and hurtful words that could never be unsaid. He spat in my face on two occasions. First time I should have kicked him to the curb, second time...game over.

NARC3- AKA "Flag Man"

The 3rd Narcissist, was my last lesson and the biggest lesson of them all.....to love myself and always trust my intuition. He is the one that nearly broke me. He gave me the courage to write this book and finally not worry what anyone else thinks about me. I'm now happy with myself and my life with my loved ones, who genuinely know me through and through. That's all that matters. Be true to yourself. I'm grateful for the lesson now. Anything is possible when you set your mind and heart to it.

In just under a year with Narc3 it ALL happened-

- GOT LOVE BOMBED -Dream holiday to the Maldives
- ENGAGEMENT – yes diamond ring indeed!
- GHOSTED
- GASLIGHTING
- FLYING MONKEYS
- BOUGHT A HOUSE TOGETHER!!
- LIES, DECEIT AND "CRAZY MAKING".
- DISCOVERED FRAUD.
- TRIANGULATION

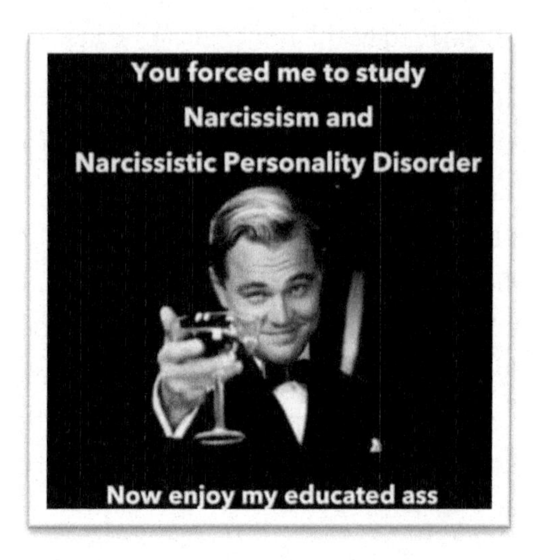

I love all these little memes! They have gotten me through a lot and I know they have helped so many out there on social media to process the whole "crazy making". And for those who are not on any social media or even use Wi-Fi, I truly hope this book helps you spot the signs and the patterns.

One online platform Quora is a very useful resource for me. One of the writers broke down covert narcissistic patterns so clearly that I have to share a bit of what they wrote. This Quora writer talks about the "invisible set up" that victims fall prey to as follows:

- **The love bomb:** "The covert narcissist love bombs in a different way than more overt narcissists. They are vulnerable, share feelings, talk about painful things. You think, "Wow! This is incredible. I've never had a relationship so deep." The covert narcissist thinks like you, shares your love languages, and inspires your compassion. You don't know how he ended up so normal when he had such a terrible family, ex, etc."

- **The façade**: "Covert narcissists are the most friendly, charming, likable people around. They help others. They're funny. They're great conversationalists and storytellers. Everyone LOVES them (except their targets)."
- **The passive aggression:** "It's the "jokes" or "teases" at first. Then the more obvious putdowns. The covert narcissist encourages you to make a decision, then punishes you for whatever you decide (there is no right answer). The sabotage is extreme and impossible to prove. They thrive on plausible deniability."
- **The Gas lighting**: "Covert narcissists are masters at distorting your reality. It's hard to fathom that someone so nice, so likeable would lie to your face. Maybe he doesn't remember the conversation? Maybe I dreamed it? He couldn't possibly have hidden my keys. You start to believe you must be going crazy. You trust his version of a story you know isn't true. You trust his memory over your own. You

start to doubt yourself about everything. You lose all connection to who you are."

- **The ultimate gas lighting**: "Because the covert narcissist is so nice, so friendly, so apologetic, so calm and because there are 1000 "loyal flying monkey" supporters, the therapists, court system, church, and larger community believe you are crazy. Your constant defending yourself against verifiable lies doesn't help. It only makes you look crazier. They look at you with pity, "If only she could find some peace."
- **The long haul:** "The covert narcissist is in it for the long haul. Many of their relationships go 10, 20, even 40, or more years. They are lazy and don't want to find new supply when they can torture you for decades."

There are so many other revelations about this form of abuse online but I find Quora to be a great source of information. The bit on the subtlety used by narcissists to lull their victims into a false sense of security, is very mind blowing. I quote below:

"The world of subtle: Just because covert narcissists do things on the subtle, it does not mean they're less harmful. In fact, they are more harmful because the victims don't even realize they are being abused. They just become more and more miserable as the life force is sucked out of them. Covert narcissistic abuse is called ***death by a thousand cuts***, for good reason."

5

YOUR ATTITUDE MATTERS

"ALWAYS BELIEVE SOMETHING WONDERFUL IS ABOUT TO HAPPEN."- **Anonymous**

In life try to turn negative situations into positive ones! No matter how difficult that sounds, if you truly believe you can do it, you will!!

I made it my mission to process all the craziness and cruel tactics endured by the man I thought I loved, the man who proclaimed to be head over heels in love with me; whose actions did not match his words. The strangest thing was, that every other day, he would be the perfect boyfriend, and the next day he would be a 55 year old toddler having a moody moment. Some days, would be dreamy and amazing. Other days, were the complete opposite. But, he made me feel like it was my fault. Deep down in my heart I knew it wasn't me, but because I thought at the time I was in love, I ignored my own intuition...my gut feeling. His "crazy making" was making me doubt myself, but I couldn't understand or describe what was happening to me.

I was drowning in the lies, the deceit, the "crazy making", the dishonesty and the fraud. At 47 years old I had two beautiful grown up children, a lovely home, a great business, and my dream car... yet I still picked the wrong man. *Was it karma? Was it me, or something*

I was doing to attract this kind of person?? All these thoughts constantly swirled around in my head.

Yes, I believe I never properly healed from the past and heart breaks. The irony is everyone who knows me personally thinks I'm so confident, cup half full kind of girl, so got it all together, always happy. I do try my very best not to put my hurt on others, so whatever happens in my life, I always do my utmost to turn every negative into a positive...my mantra since I was 14.

The fact is, I'd stopped loving myself and attracted my narcs. Not giving myself time to heal and bouncing from one long term relationship to another, was a huge mistake and a lesson I learned the hard way.

I've always had these ideal Couple goals. I always looked up to one of my friends from junior school's parents. Sadly, they have passed away now...way too young. They were my idols, I miss them dearly, a beautiful family, and one I've always strived to replicate. A loving, thoughtful, caring, respectful and beautiful relationship. I wouldn't settle just to be in a relationship, I'd have preferred to be single than in the wrong relationship. The reality, however, was that I fooled myself into thinking I had found my Prince over and over again. My reality was not lining up with my perspectives on the narcs and the life I was living with them.

For some reason, I always got attracted to the one that needed fixing. *Like attracts like*, they say, so it's shown me what I needed to work on in myself. I can see my mistakes so clearly now and going to counselling has totally transformed my life. I was holding onto a childhood trauma and now I have dealt with that. I've learnt to love myself properly, so I will maintain healthy boundaries for myself at all times.

"Although no one can go back and make a brand new start, anyone can start from now and make a brand new ending."- **Anonymous**

Mr. Right is out there, the one that doesn't need fixing, the one who loves me unconditionally...

Well I truly thought I had in 2006, until he broke my heart. Let's just say, he'd proposed, said he was planning a life together with his 4 children, my 2 children. But they never do as they say do they? We'd just got back from a holiday in Las Vegas and I found a secret Second phone in his bathroom...(flashing & vibrating while I was on the loo!!) while we were in the middle of a date night!! After reading a few texts and ranting at the cheating, lying rat, I got my things, got in my car and went back home to my house.

So what else do you do with a broken heart, feeling devastated...can't sleep, can't eat? Yep, straight into another relationship!! I had not yet learnt my lesson. I never truly healed. Instead, I tried to block it all out...like it never happened. It got really tricky when, who I thought was the love of my life at that time, came back one month later asking for my forgiveness, declaring it was the biggest mistake he'd made in his life and how sorry he was! Even though it took all my strength not to turn into mush and fall into his arms, I replied "You've made your bed, now go lay in it. I'm done, I don't do second chances." (Definitely my hurt ego talking there.!!)

As I was speaking, my new boyfriend pulls up in the drive .....Yikes ....awkward. Ever the opportunist, Mr. Cheat makes out I'm just as bad as he was. No, it was not good. It was way too quick and not fair to Mr. New.

New boyfriend turned out to be lovely to me and someone I should have probably gone on to marry...yes, he proposed too! But hey, what did silly old me go and do? Yep you got it, I went on the self-destruction route. I self- sabotaged my own happiness. I brought all the hurt from the previous relationship into this one. I was convinced he was going to do the same thing, which was not fair to him. We do speak now and he's always the perfect gentleman...still trying to protect me behind the scenes in his funny little ways.

Narc1 and Narc2 behind me, and till not having learnt my lesson; I eventually learnt from my encounter with the "Devil". Something I wouldn't wish on my worst enemy. Now I'm not putting myself in the greatest light here, but if I'm really going to show you I am worthy of writing this book, I'd like you to know a bit of my back story. I have not been an angel, I have made plenty of mistakes, lost count of my mess ups, handled some situations totally wrong, acted a total plonker at times, sometimes drank too much and hedge bounced (my party trick apparently). That being said, whenever I do something wrong, I will stand up and own that shit and apologise. The ones I love, I love with all my heart.

I feel no one has the right to intentionally lie to anyone and I've always had this strange intuition of knowing when someone is fibbing, just ask my kids, I can just see it in their eyes, can't explain it. They learnt that very young, even telling their friends at parties when they're caught out doing something they shouldn't, "don't even bother, just tell our mum the truth."

Now that I understand it more, I'm a narcissist's worst nightmare,

FLAGMAN

But let's get back to my story. Now is the time to introduce you whom I call "Flagman"- the Devil himself. Evil to the core, but you would never know unless once his mask slips. Then you will see his true colours. But to the outside world, here goes the perfect, funny, polite gentleman.

Remember what I said about gut instincts? Ignore them to your peril. .This same man had tried to take me out 2 years previously, on many occasions. My gut feeling then was, ***he's full of himself, player type, leave him where he is.*** He was on my Facebook and regularly liked and commented on random stuff and the old joke text.

Then, while I was living and working abroad, for a short time I found out his beautiful daughter had passed away from cancer at the young age of 34 and leaving 4 children behind in November 2019. I never got the privilege to meet her in person, but I did speak with her on the phone 2 years prior to her sad passing.

Today 25th November 2021 is the 2 year anniversary of her passing and I truly believe I'm meant to write this book. There is this deep urge to write it, to help others learn from my mistakes. She knew her Dad hurt people and she knew he didn't seem to care how much destruction and pain he would cause. In fact he actually still believes he's a good person. His ego is the biggest inflated ego I've ever witnessed. She guided me to all his lies early on (and actual proof) and for that

I will always be eternally grateful. Thank you Darling. The actual proof would cause his rage to go off the scale!! (Neighbours called the police to check on my well-being. He was that loud behind closed doors). When his lies were becoming more and more apparent, his rages were becoming more frequent. His web of lies were unfolding at a super-fast rate, it's like I could just look at him and see through him. It totally freaked him out and made his anger escalate to a new level. It was quite intimidating and I knew I wouldn't be safe in his company, the sooner I could escape the better.

6

SERIOUSLY! WHAT WAS I THINKING?

THE START

Narcissists are geniuses when it comes to social media, they'll make out they don't know how to use it yet they have select audience to everything they do. Take careful note of this fact!

It all started with a message of condolences. A few weeks would go by, then there was the odd message and then... a really bonkers one on a Sunday morning!

ALL RED FLAGS WERE WAVING!!! I MISSED EVERYONE!

In my defense, I knew nothing about a girlfriend up to this point as there was never any mention or photo of anyone on his Facebook. See actual message. Notice the Freudian slip with him using the word **TOXIN** by accident? Why didn't I run a mile?

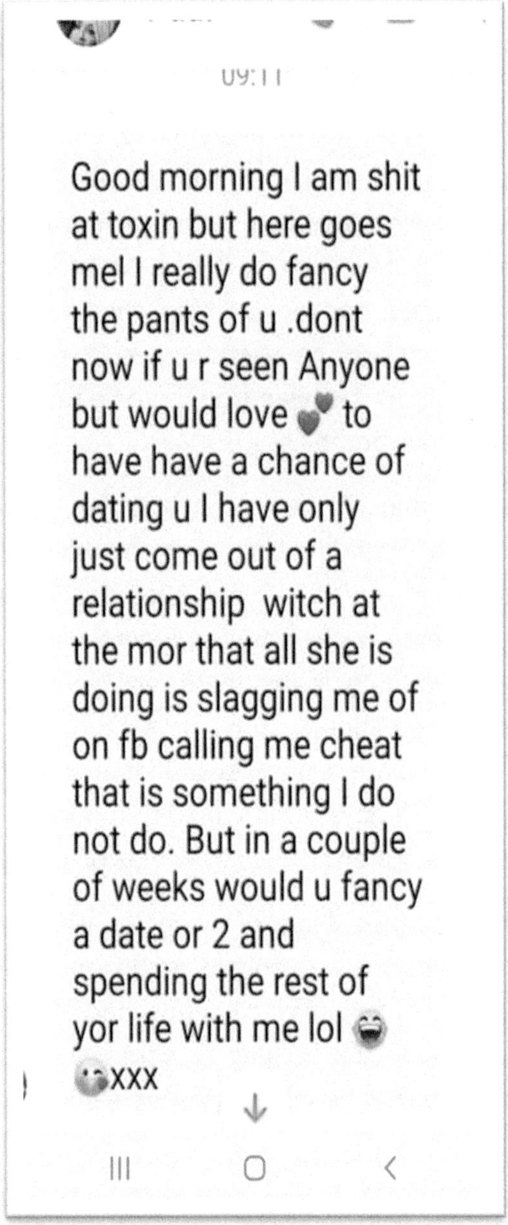

09:11

Good morning I am shit at toxin but here goes mel I really do fancy the pants of u .dont now if u r seen Anyone but would love 💕 to have have a chance of dating u I have only just come out of a relationship witch at the mor that all she is doing is slagging me of on fb calling me cheat that is something I do not do. But in a couple of weeks would u fancy a date or 2 and spending the rest of yor life with me lol 😁 😘xxx

LOVEBOMBING, which to be totally honest with you, was an amazing time. As stupid as it sounds, I thought I'd met someone with the same energy as me! Turns out, he was mirroring my every move, thoughts, likes, dislikes- same music, films, food, everything, even my energy!!. He suggested we watch a film called The Notebook (I'd never seen it). It was like a test, to see if I was emotional. And wow!! I fell for it, hook, line and sinker. Looking back he loved to watch my reaction to things, he fed off it. It was from here he really started the intense love bombing.

I remember thinking to myself***, this guy seems too good to be true, and he*** likes all some things as I do. Need to watch myself here. I should've listened to myself. There were early morning video calls, constantly wanting to be there, always wanting to know my whereabouts. But I never knew his. Then before I know it, we're booked on flights and off to the Maldives for 10 days. Who would turn down a dream holiday to the Maldives? Felt like I was on cloud nine.

Then there sudden death of his sister, which was so devastating, as she was only 56 at the time. I had only met her on 2 occasions with her husband. I thought we would postpone the holiday or something, with the funeral etc...but no he insisted we were still going.

The holiday was also booked for the 1st anniversary of his daughter's death, 25th of November 2019 and we would be in the Maldives from the 23rd November 2020 to the 2nd December 2020.

I remember feeling so sorry for his loss...***lost his daughter and sister within the space of a year and the hurt he must be going through, this man is grieving***. I'm thinking, ***is this an appropriate holiday to go on right now? Plus surely the grandchildren will need their Grandpa? His ex-wife, the grandmother of 4 children who have lost their mum and also her beloved daughter, surely she'll need support?***

RED FLAG.

Even after the death of their daughter, he and his ex-wife did not speak. Now surely after going through all that, differences would have been put aside at least for the sake of the grandchildren?

I questioned all these red flags and deep down knew something wasn't right with that situation.

When I voiced concern, I would be told he was the victim, he'd been pushed out of the funeral. Turned out he had refused to be involved, but at the time ignorant of the truth, I chose to believe him.

This is the point I should have ran away, on the plane he decides to post a picture to Facebook of the plane with the caption " let the fun begin", tagging me in on it in the process. And that is when I first saw the cold side to him... I asked him to delete it as it didn't feel appropriate, the memorial of his daughter just 2 days away. Yes, he can have his own little private remembrance while away, but Facebook really didn't sit right with me. His story was having to get away, can't deal with the grief back home, it's his life and it has made him put things in perspective, life is just way too short...

Post went up, phones went off, and then a 7 hour flight to Abu Dhabi. The minute he turned his phone back on, it literally didn't stop pinging. Then my phone started pinging. He made out the pings were from everyone wishing him a great holiday, *about time, he has found happiness etc. etc.* (no I didn't actually see these so called messages) just his version...*He's had such heartbreak with losing his daughter, his ex was crazy. Wouldn't leave him alone*.

1ST DISAGREEMENT- At the airport, he started to say his Ex was crazy, boring, (contradiction in itself) too needy you name it, he called her. Now that is a massive red flag and I said so. Something like, "please don't do that."

"What?" he asked.

"Speak badly about your Ex. At one time they were the love of your life, so why put them down now? such a waste of energy. If it didn't work, you tried, so let it go, no need to bad mouth them," I replied.

Looking back I realise how brave or stupid I was to stand up to the devil Narc. After all, I had just landed in a foreign country.

Just before boarding for Mali airport, ping, ping, ping on my phone...his Ex contacted me through FACEBOOK messenger - not just 1, not 2 but a whole load of long, messages that just kept coming. Now at that time it did make her look crazy, especially just a few minutes ago I had been sticking up for her. So my rational head kicked in, I'm about to go to my dream destination with a man who seems perfect at the time and I was determined not to let anything spoil it. Also, if I had read any of those texts (probably would have taken all week to read to be honest) it would have played on my mind. Truth, lies, jealous ex, my mind didn't know what to think...but he always had a great explanation to get around everything.

So I deleted the lot without reading any of them apart from seeing a mention of kissing his lesbian friend in a kitchen party. If only I had realised her acting crazy was his gas lighting her at every opportunity he had.

She was acting the way she was because of him and his cruel mind games, she was hurting so bad and I wish I had more knowledge at the time to see the lengths he was going to, covering his tracks and destroying people in the process.

Well, now I realise he was on a mission to claim back control, how dare I question his words. His ego was already cracking. So he went all out to make sure this was the holiday of a lifetime. Jet skis, swimming with a whale shark, romantic meals, and skinny dipping...got caught twice!! A fun loving adventure, no regrets, a lovely holiday. That's it. He mirrored me so much on that holiday, I thought I was falling in love with him, I was actually starting to love myself, I just couldn't see it until learning narcissistic patterns.

Had a lovely little memorial for his Daughter. Neither of us were sure what to do, so I suggested he write her a note, a letter and put it in a bottle and send it out to sea. Light some candles I'd brought from home. He loved the idea. So we set about finding a bottle, then realised only plastic bottles, also Maldives are islands with shallow lagoons around them. Not safe to walk in at night because of the jellyfish and baby sharks, so we walked to the end of a pier, by a beautiful fish restaurant...that was closed for the night so we had it to ourselves. It was very emotional, but something that always stuck in my mind, I was the one blubbering and breaking my heart crying 😢 thinking how much pain he must be going through, putting myself in his shoes and there was not 1 tear from him!! How could that be?

2 nights before we were due to leave, I did see an angry, sulky version of him...too much to drink. And I made excuses then. I was putting it all down to his grief. Big mistake.

7

"FUTURE FAKING"

Travelling back home from the airport, the "future faking" started. He went on and on about the amazing future we could have. He wanted us to decorate my house when we got back. There was nothing wrong with my house. In fact it's a lush home, which hadn't long been painted. But no! He insisted he wanted to treat me. In reality, he ended up paying for 1 pot of paint and half towards a new bed. I sold my sofa to a friend and bought a new one myself. But his way of manipulating situations was something else.

For example, he would say how perfect everything was, he never felt this way before, and that finally he met his soul mate...so we should never argue about money! What he really meant was he had no intention of paying for anything and there should be no discussion. So this version of a kind, considerate generous person which he projected, never ever actually showed himself.

I can recommend a great YouTube channel, Lee Hammock, "Mental Healness" who explains so much on narcissistic behaviour.

It was definitely a whirlwind romance (which hands up guilty of letting it be rushed) he was living in my house in short order. Things were amazing until he came in and heard me on the phone to a male colleague. I was laughing and joking...just being me, nothing flirty or secretive. So I held the phone away and said, "I'll be with you in a sec babe," and finished my phone call.

Well, I'm sure his eyes turned black and he snarled at me from the other side of the room.

I should have run then!

People will often ask why you did not leave a toxic relationship knowing that he/she was abusing you. Narcissists tend to covertly abuse victims. They know when to abuse and how. Some days they will be overly affectionate and some other days they will gaslight, manipulate, cheat and lie. This creates a fog in the victims mind. The victim doesn't leave because she/he is trauma bonded.

Empaths_survival

DEVALUATION

I work in a male dominated environment, but extremely lucky to set my own days and hours and a lot of my work is out on the road travelling to different locations and the rest done from my home office. He started out seeming very supportive, proud of my work and it turned into the polar opposite. So jealous, so vindictive.

He started to borrow my car...something I've worked hard for and make sure the alloys are in tip top condition. I can cover over 1000 miles in a week. Driving is a passion of mine as well as beautiful cars. And he knows this. Now I've always been generous this way and if he wanted to borrow my car, I didn't have a problem with it. The issue started when he drove it and returned it with the wheels looking like he'd spun them tightly against a curb!! To scuff all the around the wheel edge would take some doing and he denied all knowledge. In fact he said I must have done it? Total denial!

Christmas 2020 came and both families together, my Daughter, my son and his girlfriend and his son & girlfriend. Everything seemed to flow just lovely. Everyone seemed to get along.

Christmas and New Year's came and went and then the mind games began. There always seemed drama around his son's girlfriend, the son would regularly say, "Just ignore her she lies constantly."

Why on earth would he say this about his girlfriend? Even getting so-called friends *(flying monkeys)* to back up their version that she was a compulsive liar. She didn't seem to have a job and according to "Flagman" and son, "she gets a job and then gets sacked after 2 weeks."

I did notice a lot of her tall tales, of being promoted to office manager after a week, although sacked the following week. Her explanation was that her anxiety makes her unable to work. So what they were saying seemed to be true. She was the type of person who, if you've been somewhere, she's been there 3 times before. I did start to worry for her mental health as she was only 20 years old. But when you start to get the picture of who "Flagman" and son were, you could not help wondering, whether she was also being manipulated.

TRIANGULATION 1

> Triangulation consists of bringing the presence of another person into the dynamic of the relationship, whether it be an ex-lover, a current mistress, a relative, or a complete stranger. This triangulation can take place over social media, in person, or even through the narcissist's own verbal accounts of the other woman or man. The narcissist relies on jealousy as a powerful emotion that can cause you to compete for his or her affections. ~Shahadi Arabi

The mind games were relentless, which included showing me indecent photos and texts from his son's girlfriend. "Flagman" made out she had sent them to him accidentally, and then pretended he needed my advice in dealing with the situation. He asked whether I should tell his son. I immediately said yes, he should tell his son. He said it had happened a few times before and definitely no accident...plus the wrong number excuse...made no sense. *Who were they meant for? Wasn't his son obviously. And that is becoming dangerous territory; especially with the pattern of other lies, or were they?*

I was more concerned she might accuse "Flagman" of something sinister in the end. She was always asking for a lift, and he was dropping her off here and there. He insisted that I say nothing...he would sort it. So he quickly moved first asking my advice, to insisting on keeping it quiet.

I said I did notice was her behaviour was totally different in front of "Flagman" to what it was when he wasn't around and it didn't sit right with me. My kids and son's girlfriend noticed something was off too. I had to say something, express concern that it didn't feel right.

This is when I witnessed the 1st full temper tantrum...I was speechless. He flew off the handle, shouting screaming like a lunatic, grabbing his clothes and going back to his house where his son and girlfriend were living.

I literally couldn't speak at first, but when I did, he shot me down in flames. His rage was off the charts. His voice was loud naturally, so to hear him scream and shout was very intimidating at first. No reasoning, no communication...his way or no way.

I did not realise at the time that he didn't want my advice, he was only trying to make me into one of his flying monkeys against his son's ex, in case he needed one. He was simply trying to alienate her by painting her in a bad light to me.

GHOSTED.

Oki dokie...this is where I learnt about ghosting. After the incident, he literally blocked me from everywhere- Whatsapp, phone, Facebook and vanished.

A word of caution...a Narcissist always tell you what they do and what they are like in a crazy kind of way. He often said to me that he always acted poorly in relationships and that if ever he did that with me, I should just go over to his house tell him straight and he'd come straight back? When he said that, I should have run for the hills!!

Having remembered what he'd said, when he did that, I left him to it. *How dare he think it's normal, rational behaviour to speak to me or anyone like that? Plus all the blocking games. Stay gone please.*

HOOVERING.

Two weeks on' the pity texts started. *He was in a mess and needs to talk. Put it all down to his grief. The loss of his daughter and sister within one year...*and he broke down. Well, it looked that way, but there wasn't a tear. His eyes were dry.

He went on about how all the ones he loved, had passed away and he was so scared he was going to lose me too. I swear this man deserved an Oscar. What an act! But it worked on me. Empathising with his grief, I thought, *he really needs help, I'm going to help him heal...look how sorry he was. He'll never do any of that again.*

The truth is, his plan backfired. He wanted to control me, but I didn't go running after him. His plan didn't work. And looking back if it wasn't for all his suffering and grief, I would never have put up with his nonsense.

After that 1st ghosting and his subsequent false promises, he decided he'd move in properly and we were going to make a proper go of it. This is the exact point I should have spoken up and said, "NO it's too soon to move into my home."

But no, I didn't as my boundaries were weak. This is something I have since worked on for myself. He agreed to see a Grief Counselor, to help him through and control his outbursts of anger. I truly thought I could help him. Counsellor used hypnotherapy, and was the same woman I had gone to see a year before for help to give up smoking. I did stop smoking from the 1st session!!!

Although it was two different ends of the scale but I thought it was a start. He's actually addressing his issues, I thought. But not at all. His recent bereavement became his new ace card. It was his new tool for manipulating his relationships. He was now using his grief as his free pass to cause even more hurt. It was disgraceful.

8

ENGAGEMENT

"Life is too short", he would keep saying. So we made the best of every situation. We, for the most part were having a laugh, bouncing off each other, cycling, walking, off on little trips; things were great...for a very short time.

Then bam!! He bought an engagement ring from Diamond Jewelers in Amsterdam...a beautiful, stunning ring. *Maybe at 55 and everything he'd gone through he was finally going to get his life on track and be happy.* Silly of me to think that way and agree so soon, but at that time it felt so great. I was choosing to ignore the red flags and just concentrating on the good parts. In addition, there were the regular comments he would drop into our conversations, REPEATEDLY about how life is so short. Looking back I was a fool, but it has taught me valuable lessons...never trust words and to ONLY trust actions. It's pushed me to write this book to help others to spot the signs and patterns early, so they don't go through mental and emotional abuse at the hands of a Narcissist.

3 weeks went by after the engagement. He even kept joking about "happy wife, happy life." But then, enters this mate of his whom I met briefly in the beginning. He started sending odd video messages to "Flagman", video calls 1st thing in the morning...little bit of an odd thing for a man to do. So I asked, "Why don't you invite

him over for dinner, as he is your best mate. I'd like to get to know him."

He got on the offensive straight away, "Not my mate!! He's cheap labour and does work for me now and then!! Can't handle being round him. Everyone thinks he's a **** **** wannabe"

WOW! I will always remember that reaction to inviting his mate for dinner. The very brief time I had met his so-called mate, he did seem to be a bit of a "kiss ass" if you know what I mean. The little bit I had seen of him, seemed very false, but hey it was Flagman's so-called friend / work colleague, not my problem. He never invited him for dinner.

More will be revealed on this...

Tenant 1

Now "Flagman" came across as a businessman, who has done well for himself after a not so great childhood. I'm the first to congratulate and be the cheerleader at seeing people do well. I thrive on seeing lovely success stories. So he tells me he has 2 houses rented out - 1 is rented to a woman who is besotted with him, *he struggles to go there, he tends to send his son to do maintenance, because she even asked him to marry her on a valentine's day !!* So he tries not to have contact with her. Ok, I did actually giggle at first when he told me this story, but soon realised he was deadly serious (or seemed to be). As time went on that story didn't ring true, but she seemed to phone a lot.

On one occasion, we were out in the car and he pulled up at the house with me in the car. The tenant came out to the car with her grown up son. The woman (whom I've never met) just seemed to give me daggers. It was really odd but I was polite and said hello. "Flagman" didn't introduce me and the woman just said, "I know who you are."

Very odd and looking back it was probably all down to the manipulation tactics of the narcissist "Flagman" and his triangulation.

Tenant 2

This was a young lady (21 to 24) with a toddler. I first met her when I was asked by "Flagman" to produce an energy certificate for the property (my actual job and business). So there was a quick introduction and I set about doing my job, which involves going around the house in every room etc. "Flagman" arrived while I was there and behaved totally over friendly with the young lady and she seemed to act like she knew everything about him. It didn't sit comfortably with me, and my gut feeling was screaming something that didn't seem normal.

So, I mentioned it to him later that day, in a calm and rational manner. I told him how it made me feel uncomfortable and asked was there anything I needed to know about that situation. Angry outburst number 2 immediately started. He got on the defensive. *I was to blame, I was paranoid, and started screaming that something was wrong with me.* With this reaction to my question, I should have followed my gut feeling and walked away then. Hindsight is a great thing! I didn't listen, and then I chose to ignore red flags, in order to prevent the shouting and screaming...see the pattern??

The rage is to subdue us and to control us. We are the lucky ones who finally see the truth and walk away for good.

You Were Not 'Stupid'

I see survivors of abuse perpetrated
by toxic people - calling themselves stupid.
Being a normal, caring trusting person
is not being stupid.

Being conned by a master manipulator
is not being stupid.
Intelligent, caring people are conned every
day by these toxic abusers.
Please don't victim blame and victim shame
this way, either to yourself, or others.

~ Lilly Hope Lucario

I never even asked again; even though she began calling 4 or 5 times a week. Each time was a different story...her little boy had a cold, had missed nursery...nothing seemed right about it.

(Bear with me as I flick between timescales, before house purchase and after.) As our relationship developed, we decided to buy a house together. (Seriously, looking back, what on earth was I thinking!!) We lived briefly at his house where his son also lived, whilst the house purchase was going through. She called again, but this time Flagman's son was present when the call took place. She was calling about her son again, not the house she was supposedly renting. It was that he had another cold and missing nursery, so I asked "what's the score with that tenant? You'd swear the boy was your dad's the way she calls constantly."

The son's reaction and answer stuck in my mind, it was like a reflex action and erratic. "She's a complete and utter s***. Sleeps with anything, she probably doesn't even know who the father is herself. Had to kick her out of a party here for being a s***."

That response stuck in my mind and didn't sit right with me. There was definitely more to the situation.

9

THE FRAUD

Remember the lovely engagement ring he bought during lockdown, online from the Netherlands? Well that little guardian angel of mine must be on Prozac! First suspicion- I was updating his Google business page again and an email from the famous Jewelers popped up on screen while his phone was in my hand!! "Full and Final Settlement", *I read. Hmmmm...what is this?*

Now this email is months after he purchased the ring, "Why an email now?" I asked.

Straight away he snapped back that it was a postage fee refund, as he had been overcharged. I questioned how come it is only now that it is being sorted? He bought the ring months ago? His answers were plausible, but my gut was screaming at me once again. His body language was off. By then, I knew he scratched his head each time he lied, but chose to let it go.

A week later, (I swear I was being guided to his BS), I was sitting at the table in my kitchen and both our phones were sitting there. As he nipped to the loo, ping! Up on his telephone screen...the famous jeweler's email again!! This time I could see the full amount!! It was all lies, he had done an insurance job on my engagement ring! I felt sick to my stomach. Who does these things??

It turns out the delivery driver got sacked, a month before Christmas!!! I found out after I got away from him that he had told them the driver left it on the doorstep and it was stolen...my blood boils when I think about his vile ways.

He still tried to lie his way out of it...he was going to tell me when we were married. Did he think I could ever be party to that? He kept on a lot about getting married. He was in such a rush and I'm so very lucky I cancelled the one booked at the Craig y Nos Castle. I definitely had a guardian angel looking out for me because, I was just very slow in plucking up the courage to walk away for good. *But how could I look at him or the engagement ring in the same light again*? Looking back, I never truly did.

SECRET OPERATION

Usually, around 6.30am I would go downstairs, see to the dogs and make us some tea and bring them back up to bed. This particular morning "Flagman" asked me to help him with his business, as I'd set up Google business for him to grow his business. I just needed to access the app and update a few things...easy peasy...except, as he handed me his phone, a text alert in Welsh pops up...hmm strange. Yes we're both Welsh, we live in Wales, but neither of us speaks Welsh. Obviously I'm going to ask what that text is about. He declared that he had no idea, but reading his body language, he was beginning to fret. So I did a quick copy and paste into Google translate and it was a Covid test result, stating negative.

“Omg are you ok?” I ask with concern.

I also wondered why he failed to mention needing to get tested for Covid. Seemed a little strange as we live together. Straight away, he goes on the defensive and into a rage about his “bum hole” needing repairing!! Screaming on top of his voice "yeah I love cock up my arse!!!"

Cringe worthy and embarrassing, living in a semi-detached house, but I'm sure they'll put the pieces of the jigsaw together when this book comes out. My apologies for the rages they had to endure. He blamed my “paranoia” about his friendship with his mate for not telling me. This friend was sending video messages 1st thing in the morning, saying "good morning my handsome, hope you've had a lovely sleep."

Seriously I've never met men who send those messages to each other...apart from men who are gay. And if they are, they are, they are open and honest about it. That day his rage continued...screaming at me, *it is all my fault, I made him feel uncomfortable, I'm the one to blame, he doesn't feel safe to say about his operation because of me thinking his mate must be secretly gay, why else would he behave that way?*

Extreme aggression from a narcissist usually erupts when their world is about to be exposed and the truth is about to come out. No one needs to be exposed to the vile temper tantrums and word salad that comes spurting from their mouth!! To witness their eyes turn black! Believe me, anyone who has ever experienced a true narcissist will tell you the same. Their eyes in a state of pent up rage, is something you can never "unsee". They literally turn black in rage!! (Flagman's eyes are normally blue)

So you guessed what happened next. After screaming at me that no one is to know about this operation, it's private and Flagman's business only...yes you got it. He storms off with a few of his clothes, punches a hole in my wall on the way down my stairs, blocks all communication, Whatsapp, Facebook, Instagram, phone etc... GHOSTED once again.

My head was spinning, this man was not who he seems. Everything was like living on a rollercoaster. One minute high and amazing times to be had and the next feeling sick and dizzy. I felt concussed...like what's just happened? It is really not good for one's mental and emotional health feeling so up in the air, not knowing where to turn next, or what the hell has just gone on.

I didn't get out of bed for a few days. I made excuses that I wasn't feeling well. Even though I wasn't feeling right, I couldn't explain to myself let alone anyone else what I was going through. I am usually a very strong minded, get up and go kind of woman. If something drags me down, I always lift myself back up, pull my socks up, have a quick pep talk to myself in the mirror, like, "Come on girl, you got this shit, you can do this, you are stronger than you look." And I usually come back stronger than ever!

But this was feeling different. “Flagman” had drained me. I remember my son saying to me when I first introduced the “Flagman” to him, “Wow mum, you've finally met a man with the same energy as you!!”

Anyone close to me knows I always have high energy, always like to train hard, keep busy, and aim high every day at everything I put my mind to. My son’s words repeated in my head a lot over that period. I then realised that Flagman was mirroring my energy. It was NOT his to have, I realised in time...he was actually jealous of my “get up and go”.

A week later, still no sign or anything from “Flagman”. I dragged myself out for a jog around the lake by my house, had a steaming hot bath, and finished off with a jet cold shower hose down. It is a great booster. Give it a try! I did my hair and makeup, and put on a smart trouser suit; determined to drag myself out of this pity party I felt I was slipping into.

I had an amazing day, landed new freelance work, starting that week, found fantastic tenants for my house (so I could continue with my dream of renting my home out and buying another house to upgrade and sell on) pretty much like "flipping houses". All was coming together fantastically...great things really do happen when you stay away from negative people and situations. *Life is great!!*

A few weeks went by, and I was trying really hard not to think about the man I thought I was head over heels in love with. I kept telling myself, *if it was love he would never treat me the way he does, it hurts but what is meant to be will be.*

THE FORTUNE TELLER.

I remember mentioning to "Flagman" I was going to go with friends to see a fortune teller / psychic and he got really infuriated...the thought of me going along and listening to a load of crap as he put it! Yet would tell wonderful, heartwarming stories of his daughter going to see many psychics when she was alive and how much she believed in them...always a contradiction. So

I thought, *what the hell, my life, my choice, I'm off to book one.*

As it wasn't long after lockdown, psychics reading via video call, all great...told me things about family members, from both sides of my family that no one would have known, and alerted me to a family member who was feeling very down and needed help. The same family member I thought would never in a million years would be feeling down or the depressed. But later when I checked up on them it was all true what the psychic had told me, every word...they had become a recluse and I would never have known or guessed if it wasn't for them.

Then came the bit about "man in my life"- *I'm the only *woman* he has eyes for, he needs me, I can help him, and he has suffered so much trauma as a child.* They then went on about the grief he was suffering, that he needs therapy, but I will help him get it. *You are always smiling and laughing together she said, you even got the same kind of smile (which had been said before).*

Unfortunately for me, I reached out to “Flagman” to check he was OK. Seriously looking back...why on earth did I give him even a second glance (or is it 4th or 5th chance by now) after the way he had behaved? He had even convinced me I was barking mad and the bum operation was for haemorrhoids!! I didn’t know it was actually an operation. I thought it was a little procedure to tie the haemorrhoids?? I actually believed his lies!!

And WOW!! He was so happy to see me! His little plans had fallen into place. Reality of it all- when he came over to my house and realised my life was going really well, work wise and my hotpod yoga classes, enjoying a full and busy lifestyle; deep down he was raging! He didn't say it, but his actions spoke volumes. I just chose to ignore. I told him my tenants were moving in, in 3 months' time and I was on the move to look for somewhere. A normal healthy human being who says they love you, will be happy for your achievements.

Not "Flagman", he was secretly "tamping" mad at the fact, that I wasn't a nervous wreck, laid up in bed, distraught that the relationship hadn't worked out...I couldn't quite pin point it at the time, but what it boils down to is he had planned to torture me and it hadn't worked,..... yet.

He wanted in on the action, and to be part of the house move. My boundaries should have been steel and concrete barriers with an electric probe on each entrance! But hey no, my boundary walls were like candy floss!!

10

CASH MISSING

I felt I was living under a fog by this point, on a few occasions, even back at my house, I always had cash in my purse and I always knew roughly how much was in there, but the strangest things would happen, the type you can't really say out loud because it sounds crazy, nuts even. It always felt if I had 200 in my purse there would be 120 ...80 had vanished. It never even entered my head that "Flagman" could do such a thing. I always see the best in everyone. It was all too soon and too much. Another lesson learnt.

I remember being suspicious of anyone who had been in my home around that time. Now this wasn't once or twice, it was numerous times that I could never fathom. It got so bad I actually stopped carrying cash in my purse, and had a lock box in the house.

After moving to the new house my lock box started missing cash. This time I was very clear on what was happening as I always wrote the amount in there at all times, on a piece of paper. But once again I cannot prove who actually took it.

However, Flagman suddenly started to complain there was money missing from his bedside drawer!! Looked like a classic deflection, taking the focus off my instances of money going missing. Looking back, I obviously have strong views on this whole series of events.

When you tell the truth about the narcissist, remember people who have not gone through narcissistic abuse will **think you are crazy**. (Most people don't believe people like this exist.) They know only what the Narcissist wants them to see. They don't see the Person behind the mask.

To the **people** on the **outside** the **narcissist** may **appear nice, friendly** even **kind** at **times**. When you tell them that behind closed doors this person acts like a monster, not everyone is going to believe you. Don't take it personally. I know it hurts when you been through so much and you don't get support you desperately need and deserve. But its not you.

Think about before you went through this, **would you** have **understood**? Unfortunately going through Narcissistic abuse can sometimes be a very lonely experience. -Maria Consiglio

@Understandingthenarc

11

MY LIFE LESSONS

I have now learnt to unwaveringly listen to my gut feeling- my intuition. I didn't then as I believed I could help him heal, and help him with his grief...I believed his lies.

Well I'll cut to the chase. After putting a deposit on a house at auction TOGETHER and renting my house out on a year's tenancy, I temporarily moved into his house until the auction house was finalised. The son's girlfriend was long gone by this point, and I actually felt really sorry for his son. I did however over hear the son's mate say, "Let me see your dad's next victim."

He was made to lie and cover for his Dad. Even when his dad would be screaming in his face, the son would turn around the next day and say his Dad doesn't have a temper, and that he has never seen that side of him. It was like he was programmed to never speak of his Dad's vile temper. His other son could see through his BS and hadn't spoken to him in years.

I had all these questions. *Was it grief?* But it had gone too far, deposits had been paid by both of us, my home was rented out for a year. Deposits would have been lost if we backed out now.

TRIANGULATION 2.

At some point, I discovered Flag man had another life as a dog breeder. He had about 24 dogs but they were living with a certain type...similar to his so-called "best mate" but not really "his mate" kind. “Flagman” says jump, they say how high, they do all the work and keep 1 pup. He takes the money. Top marks for great business strategy, but the pattern with him calling them everything behind their backs and then sweetly sick niceness to their face; I had to speak up.

“If you can't say something nice I’d rather not hear it. You call them friends yet you take the total p*** out of them by bad mouthing them as soon as their back is turned,” I reprimanded.

Then there was the phone calls- all on loud speaker with the besotted lesbian, (that's the way it came across) who had 5 of the dogs. Depending on his moods- if he was happy with me, he would ignore her calls, and ask me to answer saying he was busy. (which I would not partake in). There were other times when we would be out for a meal and he would proceed to take calls from the same lady for half an hour (or so it seems) while I just sat there. Once I decided to give him a taste of his own medicine whilst he was in his performance and it did not end well. The rage! Storming out and back to the house, he would rage about how much money he has and they all need him. Why was I still with him again?

TIPS:

- Shouting & screaming = total waste of energy which gets you nowhere.
- Reacting to someone's temper= total lack of self- control, so walk away, don't react.
- Limit your drinking= leads to understanding your personal limits
- Walk away from toxic people.

Remember I ended up in hospital because of Narc 1? It was a very terrifying time of my life and I never spoke out about his temper and manipulation tactics behind closed doors. And he did actually make me feel crazy. I could never explain it, so I bottled most of it up. He used triangulation tactics which I did not recognise at the time when his mum said to me, "be careful you don't drink too much wine at home. Slippery slope every day."

I actually never drank wine at that time as it's really fattening. It really made me question what on earth had Narc 1 been telling his mum? Eventually, it dawned on me that he was painting a picture to establish a defense and cover up his nasty ways if ever I started to talk.

I used hindsight wisdom from my experiences with Narcs 1 & 2 to survive when I was faced with the worst of the narcs...Narc 3 aka Flagman!

Getting back to the story...Flagman's mask was slipping fast. Soon he started to scream at me for calling him by his name...I was to call him babe!! Yes! Seriously. If I answered the phone to him with "Hi" or "Hello", he would rage. I had to answer the phone in an upbeat tone (which I had all my life actually, until he appeared) then it had to be "Hello babe" in a high pitched squeal.

Where is the man I'd begun a relationship with? One day he would be absolutely lovely and the next he would be horrid. It was like being on a rollercoaster, high energy one minute, low the next, very draining. His mask was slipping and the person who appeared in his place was not the loving, caring, respectful man I'd thought he was. He was beginning to be exactly as described by the women who tried to warn me about him after the first holiday.

He was now arrogance personified. I was warned by a couple of his exes, "His ego is the size of a house and he doesn't respect women," and they told me to be careful.

Now, if I had known about Narcissistic behaviour, I would have realised exactly what those women were trying to tell me at the time. And I owe them a huge thank you for trying to forewarn me. Another lesson learnt...to stop and listen if an ex-partner or anyone who is trying to tell you something regarding a potential partner. It could potentially save a lot of wasted time and heartache.

That year, my birthday was ruined. He intentionally conjured up an imaginary offence the day before. I tried to talk to him, tried pleading with him to see there was no issue in the first place. He was only satisfied when he saw tears. I cried myself to sleep that night, waking up on my birthday feeling so confused, so drained and totally exhausted.

Never expect an explanation from a narcissist. It will never happen. He turned up at lunchtime with a card and gift voucher for a driving experience, which he took great pleasure in telling me he had the voucher a week before my actual birthday. He was laughing and joking as if everything is fine. *Nothing had happened, I'm being over dramatic, stop the nonsense, be grateful that he'd got me a card!! I'm the only woman he's ever bought a card for...*

There was never a happy medium. I felt like my head was spinning. One minute it's all laughs, jokes and happy times, the next it's nasty and evil...one extreme to the other.

I remember one shopping trip in the supermarket. I will never forgot these words...as we're doing the grocery shop together, having a laugh and a joke, nipping around the aisles “Flagman” blurts out, "I can't wait to marry you, I'm going to torture you!!"

That comment made me shiver inside. I stopped dead in my tracks and asked him, "What did you just say?"

Did I really just hear that? Am I imagining things? Why would the word torture be in the same sentence as marriage? Why on earth would he say that? He tried to play it down but he couldn't keep denying saying it...he knew I heard him.

> GASLIGHTING IS INTENTIONALLY USED TO ENSURE YOU DOUBT YOUR OWN PERCEPTION OF EVENTS. IT IS ALSO A FORM OF EMOTIONAL ABUSE USED RELIGIOUSLY BY HIGH-CONFLICT INDIVIDUALS.
>
> SARAH KAMOTO
> @NARC_PROOF_AND_THRIVING

12

"HOOVERING" & "GASLIGHTING"

TENBY

Flagman's mask was nearly completely off by this point. He was becoming frustrated as he could see me pulling away from his nonsense. He was not getting the desired reaction. He is expecting groveling at his feet, broken down by his "crazy making" behaviour, but instead I push myself to go to my hot pod yoga at 6.30am, before shower and work. I could see by the look on his face, he planned on breaking me by that point and he hadn't.

Despite all of that, I was still believing his erratic behaviour was down to his grief. And so... the extreme "hoovering" and the romantic gestures still worked. One of them was his supposed treat to spoil me with a night away in a hotel in Tenby.

Why was I surprised when arriving at the hotel, he had conveniently left his card at home? *Can I sort the bill and he'll pay it back when we're home?* At the same time he "jokes", "Ah come on you can treat us, you can afford it."

Then lo and behold as we're in the room, his card appears. No, I didn't get the money back for the hotel, but these are just a few of the manipulation games played by the narcissist. As I'm naturally a generous person, it wouldn't usually bother me as I love to spoil my loved ones. Nonetheless, I could see patterns emerging with him, and they were starting to really stand out to me.

Not one to put a damper on the night, we went out. It was a great funny night actually. We walked around the town, the harbour and on the beach, went for a meal and ended up back at the hotel. It seemed like a lovely night, he had drunk a lot more wine than me and was very drunk. So much so, that he looked like he was flirting with the male shop assistant while we were at the shops getting another bottle of wine he wanted!!

Was I imagining this? No he can't be? When I mentioned this back at the room, (actually in a jokey kind of way) "I'm sure you were just flirting with the shop assistant!?" He looked me in the face, his eyes went black and shouted on top of his voice "I love being f****d up the arse!!"

He then proceeded to Strip off, bent over and pulled the cheeks of his bum apart, repeating over and over how much he "loves cock up my arse!"

It was so disgraceful that the receptionist had a complaint and they came and knocked on the door.

By this point, apart from being totally mortified, and in shock from what I'd just heard and seen, I was speechless! I didn't even react to him, I froze, I put my head on the pillow and pretended to go to sleep. If I'd said a word, he would have just flown off into an even louder rage. He finally dropped off to sleep after an hour or so of his rants around the room.

Then, suddenly!! I'm awakened by him shaking my shoulders frantically, and shouting, "I'm going! If you want a lift get in the car now!!"

Wtf, it is 5.45am!! The room was paid for until 11am and breakfast was included. But no, he was in a vile mood and we had to leave there and then. I tried to reason with him and he just raged louder that he would leave me there if I didn't get packed straight away. I literally had minutes to pack my stuff, as he was already in the car in the car park below the window.

He didn't say a word in the car all the way back. I asked him what the hurry was. *What was wrong now? Guilt for his admission the night before?* Total silence.

Now, when we got back, his son was home in bed with one of his female friends. I immediately went upstairs, climbed into bed and went to catch up on sleep. I needed it after his temper tantrum. I felt totally drained and confused. *Was it me? Had I done something to make him behave this way?? Why is he being like this? What was the bum thing all about?* I asked myself so many questions.

But I was not allowed to go to sleep. I was in bed for probably 10 minutes, feeling totally exhausted, and very confused. In he comes telling me to get up, saying it over and over again. He was getting closer and closer to my head and repeating it in my ear. This was the 1st and last time I actually bit back to him. He had provoked me so much. The lack of sleep...it was like torture!! I started shouting back, "There is something wrong with you. You need help!! I'm out of here! I cannot be around you when you're like this. You must be gay," I shouted.

When I thought about his reaction to my querying him seeming to flirt with the male shop assistant, I could not come to any other conclusion. "You're a Closeted gay that's why you have anger issues," I told him.

This was the 1st and last time he had a reaction from me!! Looking back at the way he had set up the whole scenario, I can now tell it was for his back up story. Getting his son and one of his girlfriends to say they witnessed me shouting and calling him gay would have been priceless in discrediting me. He wanted me to look like the crazy one! This is a prime example of Gas Lighting. The thing that stood out most was the look on his face, he was so proud of himself. He'd gotten a reaction from me! It was like he was savouring every minute of it.

I can't stay under the same roof as this creature, I thought.

I have to leave and get away from him, where can I go? My house is rented out for a year, there is the new house we are supposed to have the keys to the following week. The only place I could go was my mum's house.

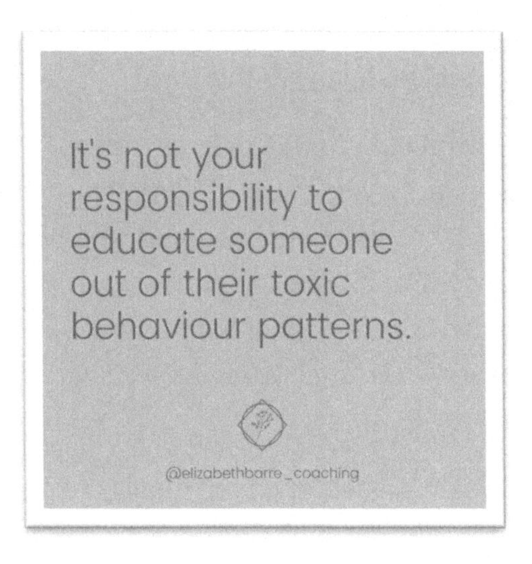

What made this very awkward was my mum's house is literally 20 houses up the street from his. As I'm packing my stuff as fast as I possibly can, he starts shouting "Get out!!"

This was intentional for his audience- his son and whichever girl he had there that day. "I'm already outta here," I told him. "You are not right in the head! That's not grief! You are mentally disturbed and if you are gay or bisexual, why don't you just admit it and come out of the Closet?? Just be honest !"

It took me 4 trips in my car, up and down the road to my mum's. He took great pleasure in breaking as much of my stuff as he could. A vase I just had for my birthday from my niece was thrown to the ground. Photo frames, were smashed to bits. I'm still finding missing or broken things to this day.

I was exhausted from lack of sleep, mentally traumatised from his crazy making, and wondering what the hell has just happened and what to do next. *Where do I go? Can't move in permanently with my mum at the age of 48, shall I go and rent somewhere till my tenants lease runs out? What to do about the new house?*

My head was in pieces, and I felt totally drained. I rang my solicitor and my mortgage guy to see what the implications would be if I pulled out then. I felt like a total fool, as they were not getting the complete picture of what was really going on. They explained it had gone too far and thousands in deposits would be lost. They reassured me that as the property didn't require drastic work, I should treat it as a purely business arrangement with Flagman. They reckoned I could get it done up within the year, put it back on the market and earn a decent profit as business partners.

Now, with a rational person that would be the light at the end of the tunnel, we had started this process so we need to complete it. But my gut feeling was screaming at me, this *man hasn't a rational bone in his body. He is jealous, needy, envious of everyone, controlling behind closed doors there would be no way on earth he would turn a negative situation into a positive one and do the house as a business venture together.*

I was by then under no illusions. It was clear to see he actually loves the highs and lows of his drama filled, circus act of a life, and having smoke blown up his ass to stroke his ego which was the size of a mansion.

I was starting to feel so disappointed in myself. How could I have been so foolish as to allow all this to happen? How couldn't I see through his nonsense earlier? I'd been so careful. I was very careful who I trusted, and not to get my home mixed up in relationships. I always made sure my kids and I had a lovely roof over our heads and now, my beautiful home is rented to lovely tenants who were hoping to rent it for years to come, my stuff is in a storage container and I'm living out of a suitcase at my mum's.

In order to avoid bumping into him, I didn't go to my mum's house as much. And if I did, I came in and went out from the top end of the road.

HOOVERING AGAIN

Then came the barrage of phone calls, the texts, and pulling up outside my mum's house. He went on about how he has messed up so bad, how sorry he was, he was scared as it's such a big step buying a house together, he was grieving. You name it, he came out with it. This part was actually all a blur to me, it was like I was on autopilot. *I was in too deep, how do I escape now?*

I mentioned to him that I'd spoken with Mortgage Company and he said he did the same. I'd put all his anger down to grief and made excuses for him on the phone to these people. I told him we'd come this far, so let's get it sorted as a business venture (which I had come to terms with in my head as too much crazy making had happened for it to be anything else). But, oh no, "Flagman" was having none of the friends business venture. Not a chance (my gut actually told me that a week prior). His words were, "we either do this as a proper couple or not at all. "

Can hear you screaming at the book right now? Run woman, now you've got chance!! I didn't even recognise myself anymore. This man had taken control of my life!! *How?? Why?? What's wrong with me?? How has he done this to me??*

Then came moving day. Any guesses where he disappears to?? Big golf game on the 1st morning in the new house. His words, "start as you mean to go on. Happy wife happy life."

13

ALL IS REVEALED!
I AM NOT GOING CRAZY!

The longer we were at the house together, the easier it was for me to spot the manipulation. Remember his so called friend (who was never invited to dinner as he said he wasn't his friend) and when Flagman went mental saying he was just cheap labour? Well, AFTER moving into our home, in at least one in 3 (of his now frequent rages) he would blurt out, "You'd better get used to "******" coming over as he's my best friend and work needs doing on this house!"

I learnt not to react, not to bite because that is exactly what he wanted...a reaction.

On the 2 occasions he (best friend) came to the house, the same thing happened as happened the 2 times I had visited his house with Flagman. I FELT PHYSICALLY SICK and I couldn't explain it. It was so strange but this feeling was overwhelming. The first time it happened, I thought I had food poisoning or something and as I left his house the feeling eased...it was very surreal.

The evening before all was unveiled, HE was there, the feeling of sickness started and I made an excuse to say I was taking the dogs out in the car. I just had to get away. I got back to the house, not much carpentry work had been completed, in fact hardly anything, but I made them both food and tried to stop myself from throwing up.

Still baffled by what was happening to me, and to some extent, being unwilling to admit what was staring me in the face, I just played along. My own intuition was screaming at me, and I chose to ignore it!!

The following morning we were laughing and joking, I had made us tea & breakfast in bed as usual. I was trying so hard to make the best of this crazy situation, but I really couldn't make head or tail of what was really going on.

I made a comment about the night before, “What do we owe for the work?"

A joint bank account was set up for the work done on the house. His reply was, "nothing".

Me being me said, “You can't not pay him for his time, he has to be paid something?”

0-100mph in seconds, off the scale lunatic banshee mode...he went ballistic! “He does it for free!" He was screaming, shouting, and hurling abuse at me. The more hurtful the words were, the better he felt. He thrived on the hurt he would inflict.

There was a pattern as his son fitted a brand new gas boiler free of charge also. It took hours of his time each day for 5 days to do, but everything is expected to be free in the eyes of “Flagman”. The screaming and shouting of abuse continued, but I didn't even react to him. I realised he was always seeking, a reaction.

It got worse! Suddenly, he threw his breakfast plate at me, but it missed me and hit my little dog (the photo you saw earlier) she's my little angel. Lost her 6 times as a puppy through fitting, so obviously I'm going to protect her with my life. She was screaming in pain! And "Flagman" did nothing, no reaction, nothing. I was trying to console my dog, and see what damage he had inflicted on her, whilst he was still raging like a lunatic!!

That spoke volumes, because a normal, rational human being, wouldn't throw a plate in the 1st place. Secondly, they would stop in their tracks after hearing the screams of a defenseless dog!! But hey no, he just continued with his rage.

WAKE UP CALL!!

Seeing his reaction to what he had just done to my little Pomeranian dog, it totally woke me up. I had seen enough of his disgusting ways, lies, and deceitfulness. I just had to get away, house or not. So I waited for him to leave. I didn't react to anything he screamed or shouted. I went Grey-rock and the minute he left, I packed my stuff and left there to go and stay with my mum.

It was overdue. I should have left 3 weeks before. I had been asked by him to sort his Google business page and on having his phone for literally seconds, I discovered a dating app profile page! He was adamant it wasn't him, he had no idea how it was there, and it magically appeared!! Unbelievable, but true.

He then did his usual...storms off to his house with son, comes back, tail between legs. As a confident independent woman, I'd said to him in the past, that any person who needs to play detective in a relationship, is in the wrong relationship. He rightly believed I would never look at a man's phone. So to beg for forgiveness, after this incident, he gave me his Facebook, email, and messenger passwords. I called his bluff and got him to log into them all on my tablet. I saw no evidence of foul play... listening to this back now, I really want to shake myself rigorously.

So fast forward, I am back at my mum's after he'd hurt my dog, and I remembered...***all his accounts are on my tablet from 3 weeks ago! I want answers! Something doesn't add up! I want the truth!!***

Lo and behold, within 10 minutes of snooping!! It was all there in black and white!! He is a Closeted, covert narcissist!

Finally, I had proof that my gut feeling never lied to me and all along, my intuition was always correct. I was the fool not to listen to it. I could not understand why he would have his 3 weekly tantrums and leave for a while. Now it made sense. He wanted time with his boyfriend. Why can't people just be honest?? Is that really too much to ask? There would be a hell of a lot less drama if people just told the truth.

The following day, after taking in all I discovered on my tablet about Flagman, I went back to the house and made sure he would be the one to leave. My home was rented out on a year's lease, his house was fine for him to go back to. So, I would live at the house with my dog.

The following morning he turned up again at the house, banging on the door!! He started accusing me of having someone in the house demanding to search the attic to prove it! Then he swung to begging me for another chance, telling me he was not gay, "the messages are dodgy but I'm not gay".

If only he was honest and could own up to the fact that he is bisexual and probably has been all his life. But no, even at the age of 55 he wanted to masquerade in the circus that he calls his life, to pretend to the outside world he is a straight man. I can only imagine that the hate he seems to have for women is rooted in the resentment he feels for his mother whom he said was cruel to him as a child.

Somehow, it appears he feels entitled to play mind games with women, because of the abuse from his mother. That is where my pity stops for him, because there are millions out there who have had terribly awful childhood experiences, but they choose to make their life better. But the narcissist takes pleasure from intentionally hurting and destroying the ones they pretend to care for.

Why did they try to destroy you?

Because the darkness in them
recoils from your light.

Their empty heart resents
your abundant love,
and their strange hunger
feeds on the pain they cause.

Your resilience enrages them.
Despite doing their worst,
they could never break you.

They hate you because
they are something monstrous,
and you are nothing like them.

Anonymous

Finally realising I'm onto all his mind games, frauds and total crazy making, his anger kicks in again, smashing up the kitchen that was to replace the fitted kitchen and throwing it onto the back of his van! I didn't react, so he drags my watch off my wrist! I didn't react! He then takes the blue eyed, panda looking puppy out of my hands, I didn't react!

He notched it up another level and starts screaming on top of his voice, "How mental are you? I've shown all my friends the gay" texts and they reckon nothing wrong with them!"

More lies & control. Continuing he screams, "That ginger f*****g kid with the ginger slag, the kid is mine!" Remember the tenant no.2 lady? Seriously, he was trying the most pathetic rages to get me to react to him and I never ever did or never have to this day. I just see a cold shell with a very ugly heart.

CONTROL

Having had no response or change from me, he refused to let me buy his share in the house. Therefore, could not decorate the house and make it my home. For over a year, I lived in a ripped apart house. I decorated my office and bedroom. Those 2 rooms are lovely and that will do me until I can get back to my lovely beautiful home and away from the narcissist forever. This experience has also given me the strength and no excuses to actually write this book to help others spot the signs early and hopefully spot the red flags.

I'm now happy to be free from his lies and the circus he calls his life and his controlling sick mind games. It's always about control with him and not allowing me to buy his share, is his ultimate form of control.

Some of the lessons I have learnt:

- To walk away if my intuition tells me to. GUT NEVER LIES!!
- Don't sweat the small stuff!!
- To take the time to heal properly from any childhood traumas.
- Not to dig my heels in to prove the lies - it's not worth the pain of proving the truth, I already know.

I'm a truth seeker! But I am always thinking I can help and fix people. But I cannot. You cannot fix anyone. They will destroy you first.

As you gain confidence in yourself, red flags are no longer red flags. They are dealbreakers.

To conclude, what I had to do to help myself to heal from my sojourn with narcissists, was watch multiple YouTube videos on the topic, and read loads of articles on Quora. I listened to podcasts and anything I found to gain knowledge. I found a lot of the information helped me so much to understand *I wasn't going crazy...this really does go on in life. I was even more* shocked to see how many others there are out there. Some have been going through it for years, having nowhere to turn. So many have been beaten down for years, with no one to talk to, or confide in.

I no longer feel crazy. He tried so many times to make me believe that was true. He did a number on me with his double standards and cruel words behind closed doors. I learnt to regain my strength inside and out and to start believing in ME again. I now truly love myself.

This is the reason I will donate 20% of the sales of my book to a charity that can help victims of coercive behaviour. And if there isn't one available, I will make it my mission to build a charity from scratch.

So thank you "Flagman", you have taught me my biggest lesson in life...always listen to my gut...it always tells me the truth. I could have saved so much time and heartbreak if I had stopped and listened to my own intuition sooner. Hopefully you will learn from my mistakes or be able to help a friend or loved one to escape from a narcissistic relationship after reading this. Believe them always.

Find my “15 Step Road to the New You” to help you on your healing journey for the trauma from narcissistic abuse on my Instagram page @narcissistic_patterns.

Be Safe Darling,

Thank You

Mel

X

ABOUT THE AUTHOR

Melanie John is a 49 year old mother of two young adults, now 27 and 21 years of age. Born and bred in Swansea, South Wales, she runs her own business as a freelance Retrofit & Energy Assessor. A self-proclaimed tomboy, she is licensed to drive Lorries and motorbikes, but her passion is cars and road trips to beautiful destinations.

Having suffered at the hands of 3 narcissists, she now makes it her mission to help others spot the signs and red flags through her Instagram page @narcissistic_patterns. Even if it helps one person to take their time and really get to know someone (before committing to a relationship) and not fall for false promises. Mel believes it is vital to only trust in someone's actions (over a period of time) and NEVER just their words.

Printed in Great Britain
by Amazon